Editor in Chief
Ina Massler Levin, M.A.

Creative Director
Karen Goldfluss, M.S. Ed.

Illustrator
Kelly McMahon

Cover Artist
Barb Lorseyedi

Art Coordinator
Renée Christine Yates

Imaging
Leonard P. Swierski

Nonfiction & Fiction Reading Comprehension

GRADE 1

Practice Makes Perfect

Contributing Authors
Ruth Foster, M. Ed.
Eric Migliaccio

Publisher

Mary D. Smith, M.S. Ed.

Teacher Created Resources, Inc.
6421 Industry Way
Westminster, CA 92683
www.teachercreated.com
ISBN: 978-1-4206-3028-2

© 2010 Teacher Created Resources, Inc.
Made in U.S.A.

Teacher Created Resources

Table of Contents

Introduction 3

Practice Pages
(In order, the practice pages include a nonfiction story, a fiction story, and a set of five questions about the stories.)

1. *Stories:* "You and Tigers" and "A Warning Tail" 4

2. *Stories:* "Shark Teeth" and "The Missing Teeth" 6

3. *Stories:* "Building a Bridge" and "The Ant Boat" 8

4. *Stories:* "Swimming Across" and "A Swimmer's Diary" 10

5. *Stories:* "An Island State" and "Ski Two Ways" 12

6. *Stories:* "The Left-Handed Pitcher" and "Pitch, Catch, and Throw" 14

7. *Stories:* "The Low Land" and "A Giant Thinker" 16

8. *Stories:* "A Place to Put Stuff" and "Aunt Patty's Pocket" 18

9. *Stories:* "The Smell of Danger" and "Mystery at the Beach" 20

10. *Stories:* "The First Step" and "Jumping Jacky" 22

11. *Stories:* "All Over the Earth" and "The Wet Hat" 24

12. *Stories:* "Twisting Your Tongue" and "Food for Thought" 26

13. *Stories:* "An Author's Guests" and "Out of Sight" 28

14. *Stories:* "Four Thumbs and a Pouch" and "Pizza for Breakfast" 30

15. *Stories:* "A Snowy Save" and "The Free Ride" 32

16. *Stories:* "Fresh from the Ocean" and "A Letter About Long Ago" 34

17. *Stories:* "Everything Floats" and "A Tricky Egg" 36

18. *Stories:* "The Chinese New Year" and "The Red Doors" 38

19. *Stories:* "Sailing Across Land" and "Birds that Swim" 40

20. *Stories:* "Saved by the Bell" and "The Country Horses" 42

21. *Stories:* "Archie's Pet" and "The Monster Upstairs" 44

22. *Stories:* "Reading with Fingers" and "Reading in the Dark" 46

Answer Key 48

Introduction

The old adage "practice makes perfect" can really hold true for your child and his or her education. The more practice and exposure your child has with concepts being taught in school, the more success he or she is likely to find. For many parents, knowing how to help their children may be frustrating because the resources may not be readily available.

As a parent, it is also difficult to know where to focus your efforts so that the extra practice your child receives at home supports what he or she is learning in school.

This book has been written to help parents and teachers reinforce basic skills with children. *Practice Makes Perfect: Nonfiction & Fiction Reading Comprehension* gives children practice with reading and answering questions that help them fully comprehend what they have read. The inclusion of both a nonfiction article and a fictional story for each set of questions gives children practice with reading, comparing, and contrasting two related—but fundamentally different—written pieces.

The exercises in this book can be done sequentially or can be taken out of order, as needed. After reading the stories, children will answer most of the questions by filling in bubbles on the question pages. This gives them practice with answering questions in the format of many standardized tests.

The following standards or objectives will be met or reinforced by completing the practice pages included in this book. These standards or objectives are similar to the ones required by your state and school district and are appropriate for first grade:

- The student will demonstrate competence in what is read.

- The student will demonstrate competence in understanding how print is organized.

- The student will demonstrate competence in using various reading strategies to read the stories and answer the questions.

- The student will demonstrate competence in finding the story's main idea, making inferences, and making predictions.

- The student will demonstrate competence in beginning to recognize different types of reading (e.g., fiction, nonfiction)

How to Make the Most of This Book

Here are some useful ideas for making the most of this book:

- Set aside a specific place in your home to work on this book. Keep this area neat, tidy, and stocked with needed materials.

- Establish consistency by setting up a certain time of day to work on these practice pages.

- Keep all practice sessions with your child positive and constructive.

- Read aloud with your child and participate by asking the comprehension questions.

- Review the work your child has done. Pay attention to the areas in which your child has the most difficulty. Provide extra guidance and exercises in those areas.

- Allow your child to use a special writing instrument if he or she prefers. For example, colored pencils can add variety and pleasure to drill work.

You and Tigers

Look at your thumb. It has lines on it. These lines are your thumbprint. Your thumbprint is your own. No one else has a thumbprint like yours. Your thumbprint tells who you are.

Look at a tiger's face. It has stripes on it. A tiger's face is like your thumbprint. How can a tiger's face be like your thumbprint?

Each tiger has its own stripe pattern. No other tiger has the same stripe pattern. A tiger's stripe pattern tells which tiger it is.

A Warning Tail

Annie said, "Look at that tiger's tail. A friendly tiger puts its tail up. It slowly wags it back and forth. That tiger's tail is not up. It is not wagging slowly back and forth."

James said, "You are right! That tiger's tail is not high at all. It is low. It is twitching from side to side."

Annie said, "That means the tiger is tense. It is telling everyone to be careful. It is warning us to watch our step."

James said, "I will tell you something with words, not a tail. I'm glad that tiger is in the zoo and not out here with us!"

Directions: Fill in the bubble next to each correct answer.

1. **What is true about a tiger's face stripes?**
   - (A) No other tiger has a pattern like it.
   - (B) It has the same pattern as other tigers.
   - (C) Some other tigers have a pattern like it.
   - (D) It has the same pattern as your thumbprint.

2. **If a tiger's tail is up high and wagging slowly back and forth, that means the tiger is**
   - (A) tense.
   - (B) friendly.
   - (C) telling everyone to be careful.
   - (D) warning you to watch your step.

3. **What do both stories have in common?**
   - (A) They are both about tails.
   - (B) They are both about prints.
   - (C) They are both about tigers.
   - (D) They are both about patterns.

4. **Look at the picture on the left. Find the matching thumbprint pattern on the right.**

5. **Look at the picture to the right. Which story does it show?**

   - (A) "You and Tigers"

   - (B) "A Warning Tail"

Shark Teeth

Sharks have lots of sharp teeth. Sharks have powerful jaws. With their sharp teeth and powerful jaws, sharks can bite hard. They can bite through steel!

Sharks lose their teeth all the time. Their teeth fall out every time they bite something hard. You don't lose teeth all the time. You only lose your baby teeth. This is because your teeth are set firmly into your jaw. A shark's teeth are not set firmly in its jaw.

Your teeth take a long time to grow in. Shark teeth grow in fast. A shark's tooth can grow back in just one day!

The Missing Teeth

Paul had two loose teeth. He liked to wiggle his loose teeth with his tongue. He wiggled those teeth back and forth for three days.

On the fourth day, Paul bit into a hard apple. After his first bite, he tried to wiggle his teeth with his tongue. His teeth were missing! Where did they go?

Paul yelled, "Help! Help! My teeth are gone!"

Paul's father and sister came running. They looked in Paul's mouth. They looked on the floor. They could not find the missing teeth. Then Paul's sister laughed. She pointed at Paul's apple. "Look!" she said. "Your teeth are stuck in the apple!"

Directions: Fill in the bubble next to each correct answer.

1. What is true about shark teeth?

(A) They are not sharp.

(B) The do not grow in fast.

(C) They do not fall out easily.

(D) They are not set firmly in its jaw.

2. How many loose teeth did Paul have at the beginning of the story?

(A) 1   (C) 3

(B) 2   (D) 4

3. Most likely, if something is firmly set,

(A) it can wiggle.   (C) it cannot wiggle.

(B) it cannot grow back.   (D) it cannot bite hard.

4. Look at the parts of the story written in the boxes. What's missing?

Paul had two loose teeth. → [ ] → Paul's teeth were stuck in the apple.

(A) Paul's teeth grew back.   (C) Paul bit into an apple.

(B) Paul's father found the teeth. (D) Paul finished eating his apple.

5. Look at the picture to the right. Which story does it show?

(A) "Shark Teeth"

(B) "The Missing Teeth"

Building a Bridge

Deep in the jungle, ants are marching. The ants are army ants. They are looking for food. They come to a place they cannot cross. What can the army ants do to get across?

The ants know just what to do. Some of them link their legs together. They form a strong chain. The chain stretches like a bridge to the other side. It is a bridge made up of army ants. It is a bridge that is alive!

Other ants walk across the chain. They cross to the other side. Then, they continue to march. They keep on marching deep into the jungle.

The Ant Boat

Max was in a rainy jungle. A guide was leading his group. The ground was flooded. Water was everywhere. Max saw something strange. It was floating in the water.

"Don't touch!" cried Max's guide. "That floating thing is alive!"

Max was puzzled. What could the strange thing be?

The guide said, "It is a bunch of ants. The ants have joined together so they are like an 'ant boat.' As the 'boat' floats, it rolls over and over. The ants go in and out of the water. The 'boat' keeps them from drowning. They do not drown because they breathe when they roll out of the water."

Directions: Fill in the bubble next to each correct answer.

1. The ants make a chain by

Ⓐ continuing to march.

Ⓑ marching deep in the jungle.

Ⓒ linking their legs together.

Ⓓ stretching to the other side.

2. A guide

Ⓐ is a bunch of ants.

Ⓑ shows visitors around.

Ⓒ is a boat that is alive.

Ⓓ joins visitors together.

3. Most likely, the ants make an "ant boat"

Ⓐ when they are puzzled.

Ⓑ when they are looking for food.

Ⓒ when they want to cross the jungle.

Ⓓ when the jungle floods so they do not drown.

4. Which group of ants has their legs linked together?

Ⓐ

Ⓑ

Ⓒ

5. Look at the picture to the right. Which story does it show?

Ⓐ "Building a Bridge"

Ⓑ "The Ant Boat"

Swimming Across

The wind was strong. The water was choppy. Ships were told not to cross the channel. It was not safe.

Gertrude Ederle was in the water. She wanted to swim from France to England. A channel of water is between the two countries. It is called the English Channel. Gertrude was trying to swim across the English Channel.

Gertrude's trainer was in a boat. He saw that the water was choppy. He was afraid Gertrude would get hurt. He told Gertrude that she should get out of the water.

Gertrude stayed in the water! She did not stop swimming. She swam across the English Channel. She was the first woman to swim from France to England.

Fiction

A Swimmer's Diary

August 5, 2010

Dear Diary,

Tomorrow I will try to swim from France to England! At last, I will try to do what my hero did. Gertrude Ederle is my hero. She was the first woman to swim across the English Channel. She swam it on August 6 in 1926.

I will be like Gertrude. I will coat my skin with lard. Lard is fat. The lard will help me stay warm. It will help protect me from the icy water.

August 6, 2010

Dear Diary,

I did it! I swam to England! I swam across the channel like my hero!

Directions: Fill in the bubble next to each correct answer.

1. **Why did Gertrude's trainer tell Gertrude she had to get out of the water?**

   Ⓐ He wanted Gertrude to be safe.

   Ⓑ He wanted Gertrude to be first.

   Ⓒ He wanted to be Gertrude's trainer.

   Ⓓ He wanted to go from France to England.

2. **How many days in the swimmer's diary did you read about?**

   Ⓐ 1   Ⓒ 3

   Ⓑ 2   Ⓓ 4

3. **Most likely, Gertrude did not wear a wet suit to stay warm because**

   Ⓐ wet suits had not been invented yet.

   Ⓑ her trainer told her to use a wet suit.

   Ⓒ she knew later swimmers would want to use lard.

   Ⓓ wet suits protect against icy water better than lard.

4. **It's time for a scavenger hunt! Find each of these things in "A Swimmer's Diary." Write your answers in the boxes.**

the name of a month	the name of a year	the name of a country

5. **Look at the picture to the right. Which story does it show?**

   Ⓐ "Swimming Across"

   Ⓑ "A Swimmer's Diary"

An Island State

Hawaii is a state. It is one of the United States. There are 50 states. Hawaii became a state in 1959. It became the 50th state.

Hawaii is made up of islands. The biggest island is the "Big Island." The Big Island is getting bigger. It is growing! How can this be?

There are volcanoes on the island. The volcanoes erupt. Hot lava flows out. The lava cools. It gets hard. This makes new land.

People visit Hawaii. They go to the beach. They lie in the sun. They dig in the sand. They play, swim, surf, and fish.

Ski Two Ways

Ken moved to Hawaii. Megan said, "Ken, I will take you skiing tomorrow."

In the morning, Megan took Ken to the beach. They went water skiing. Then Megan said, "Get your coat. We are going to ski some more."

Ken said, "Why will I need a coat to ski?"

Megan said, "We are going to ski on snow! We are going to ski down Mauna Kea's slopes. Mauna Kea is a volcano. The top slopes of the volcano are covered in snow."

Ken said, "I like this state! I can ski in two different ways all on the same day!"

Directions: Fill in the bubble next to each correct answer.

1. Hawaii became a state in

(A) 1989.

(B) 1979.

(C) 1969.

(D) 1959.

2. What did Megan tell Ken to get?

(A) his skis

(B) his coat

(C) his slope

(D) his volcano

3. From the stories, you can tell that Ken did not know that

(A) there was snow in Hawaii.

(B) Hawaii was the last state.

(C) there were beaches in Hawaii.

(D) Hawaii was made up of islands.

4. What information about Hawaii belongs in the middle box?

Volcanoes erupt.		The lava cools.

(A) Hawaii is a state.

(B) People visit Hawaii.

(C) Hot lava flows out.

(D) Hawaii is made up of islands.

5. Look at the picture to the right. Which story does it show?

(A) "An Island State"

(B) "Ski Two Ways"

The Left-Handed Pitcher

Jim Abbott was born without a right hand. Kids were mean to Jim. They called him names. Jim wanted to play baseball. He did not let anything stop him.

People said, "You won't go far." Jim proved them wrong. He just kept practicing. He practiced pitching with his left hand. He practiced slipping his glove on and off of his left hand. He practiced catching with his left hand.

Jim's practice paid off. Jim became a great baseball player. He went to the Olympic Games in 1988. He helped his team win the gold medal. Then, he turned pro. Jim played a long time in the pros. He won 87 games. He even pitched a no-hitter!

Pitch, Catch, and Throw

Tim was watching a baseball game. "Dad," said Tim in surprise, "the pitcher has only one hand! How can he pitch, catch, and throw?"

Tim's Dad said, "That's Jim Abbott. Watch how he does it."

Tim saw Jim pitch with his left hand. Jim held his glove in the crook of his right elbow. Jim slipped the glove on his left hand after pitching.

Tim saw Jim catch a ball. Jim cradled the glove and ball in the crook of his right elbow. He grabbed the ball with his left hand and threw it. Jim did all of this very quickly.

Tim said, "He's not just one-handed! He's fast!"

Directions: Fill in the bubble next to each correct answer.

1. How did Jim become such a good baseball player?

Ⓐ He practiced.

Ⓑ He turned pro.

Ⓒ He won a gold medal.

Ⓓ He won 87 games.

2. When Jim pitched, where did he hold his glove?

Ⓐ in his left hand

Ⓑ in his right hand

Ⓒ in the crook of his left elbow

Ⓓ in the crook of his right elbow

3. What do both stories have in common?

Ⓐ mean kids

Ⓑ a pitcher

Ⓒ the Olympic Games

Ⓓ Tim and his dad

4. Write below each hand if it is the palm (front) of a left hand or a right hand.

_ _

5. Look at the picture to the right. Which story does it show?

Ⓐ "The Left-Handed Pitcher"

Ⓑ "Pitch, Catch, and Throw"

The Low Land

The Netherlands is a country. Much of the land is low and flat. This land is so low, it is below sea level. The Netherlands is close to the sea. So why isn't the land under water? Why isn't the land flooded?

People in the Netherlands made dikes. A dike is a kind of dam. The dikes in the Netherlands are like low walls.

First, the people built dikes around an area. They built canals, too. Then, the people pumped out the seawater from the land inside the dikes. The seawater ran through the canals. It ran back into the ocean. This is why the Netherlands does not flood.

A Giant Thinker

A mean giant dumped a huge pile of dirt in the river. The dirt made a dam. The dam stopped the water.

The giant roared, "I am big and strong! You can't move all that dirt! You will never get water to your village!"

Allie said, "I can get the water to go to my village." Allie took a little spoon. She dug a tiny gap across the top of the dam. Water began to flow slowly through the gap. Then it began to flow faster and stronger.

Allie said, "I am small and weak, but I can think."

Directions: Fill in the bubble next to each correct answer.

1. **What is *not* true about land in the Netherlands?**

   Ⓐ It is low.   Ⓒ It is flooded.

   Ⓑ It is flat.   Ⓓ It is below sea level.

2. **Allie did not have to move all the dirt because**

   Ⓐ the dam was tiny.   Ⓒ she only had a little spoon.

   Ⓑ she was small and weak.   Ⓓ the water flowed through a gap.

3. **What did you read about in both stories?**

   Ⓐ dams   Ⓒ canals

   Ⓑ giants   Ⓓ sea water

4. **The words "hot" and "cold" are opposites. Write down the opposites from the story "A Giant Thinker."**

   • huge _____

   _____

   • small _____

   _____

   • strong _____

   _____

5. **Look at the picture to the right. Which story does it show?**

   Ⓐ "The Low Land"

   Ⓑ "A Giant Thinker"

A Place to Put Stuff

Look at your pants. Does it have pockets? Long ago, pants did not have pockets. How did you think people carried things? Where did they put their stuff? They used a pouch. The pouch hung from a loop. The loop was on a belt.

Pockets were first made in the 1600s. The first pockets did not look like the ones we have today. The first pockets were like pouches. They hung outside the pants.

Inside pockets were not invented until the 1700s. Today, many pants have pockets. Some have lots of pockets. How many pockets does your favorite pair of pants have?

Aunt Patty's Pocket

Aunt Patty said, "Lucy, I have a fun riddle for you. It might be hard. Let's see if you can answer my riddle."

Lucy said, "I like hard riddles. Ask me yours!"

"Okay," said Aunt Patty. "I have something in my pocket. But I am not carrying anything in my pocket. What is in my pocket if I am not carrying anything?"

Lucy said, "That is a hard riddle. But I think I can solve it! Is the answer 'a hole'?"

"Yes, good for you!" cheered Aunt Patty. "But that's not so good for me. I have a hole in my pocket!"

Directions: Fill in the bubble next to each correct answer.

1. **When were inside pockets for pants invented?**

   (A) in the 1600s   (C) in the 1800s

   (B) in the 1700s   (D) in the 1900s

2. **Aunt Patty could not carry anything in her pocket because**

   (A) she had a riddle.   (C) her pocket had a hole.

   (B) Deb had something fun.   (D) Deb could answer the riddle.

3. **From the stories, you can tell that**

   (A) pockets were invented before riddles.

   (B) riddles were invented before pockets.

   (C) pockets were invented before pouches.

   (D) pouches were invented before pockets.

4. **Unscramble the letters to spell out the answer to the riddle.**

   Riddle: **Which side of a cheetah has the most spots?**

   Unsramble these letters: **u t o**

   _____

   - - - - - - - - - - -
   Answer: **the** _____ **side!**

5. **Look at the picture to the right. Which story does it show?**

   (A) "A Place to Put Stuff"

   (B) "Aunt Patty's Pocket"

Nonfiction

The Smell of Danger

A person went to the beach. He dug for clams. He put his clams in a bucket. He was going to take the clams home. He was going to cook and eat them.

The person started to leave. A big dog ran up. The dog put its nose right by the bucket. The dog barked. It barked and barked.

The dog was a police dog. The dog was trained to smell clams. The clams in the bucket were not safe! Something in the water had made the clams unsafe to eat. The police dog kept the person from getting sick.

Fiction

Mystery at the Beach

"Mmm! Those hot dogs smell good!" said Pam. Pam's family was having a picnic at the beach. They were cooking hot dogs.

Just then Pam's brother said, "Look up! There is a hot-air balloon in the sky!"

Everyone looked up at the hot-air balloon. When they looked down, they did not see something. The hot dogs were gone! No one knew where the food had gone. It was a mystery.

At the other end of the beach, a lady said, "What is wrong with the dog? He doesn't seem hungry. It is a mystery why he's not hungry."

Directions: Fill in the bubble next to each correct answer.

1. **What did you read about in both stories?**

   Ⓐ a hungry dog   Ⓒ a dog at a beach

   Ⓑ what a dog ate   Ⓓ a dog that barked

2. **Most likely, where did the hot dogs go?**

   Ⓐ Sally ate them.   Ⓒ The lady ate them.

   Ⓑ The dog ate them.   Ⓓ Sally's brother ate them.

3. **When you don't know why or how something happens, it is a**

   Ⓐ clam.   Ⓒ balloon.

   Ⓑ police.   Ⓓ mystery.

4. **Three people talked in the story "Mystery at the Beach." Draw lines to show the order in which people spoke. The first line is drawn for you.**

   1st   a lady on the beach

   2nd   Pam

   3rd   Pam's brother

5. **Look at the picture to the right. Which story does it show?**

   Ⓐ "The Smell of Danger"

   Ⓑ "Mystery at the Beach"

The First Step

Neil Armstrong stepped out of the *Eagle*. It was July 20, 1969. Neil went where no person had ever gone before. He stepped onto the moon. He was the first person to do that.

Neil left a flag on the moon. It was the flag of the United States. A thin wire was sewn on the flag. This thin wire held the flag out.

Neil left his footprints on the moon, too. Neil's footprints are still there. Why are Neil's footprints still there? On the moon, there is no wind. There is no rain. Nothing will blow or wash his footprints away.

Jumping Jacky

My name is Jacky. I live on the moon. My address is Moon Base 6. I have to wear a spacesuit outside the station. This is because there is no air on the moon.

I like to jump and play on the moon. I can jump really high. This is because there is less gravity on the moon. People weigh less when there is less gravity.

On the moon, I am very light. I only weigh about 8 pounds (4 kg)! On Earth, I would weigh about 50 pounds (23 kg). It must be very hard to jump on Earth.

Directions: Fill in the bubble next to each correct answer.

1. Both stories are about

Ⓐ being on the moon. Ⓒ gravity on the moon.

Ⓑ jumping on the moon. Ⓓ spacesuits for the moon.

2. Jacky can jump higher on the moon than she can on Earth because

Ⓐ her spacesuit makes her weigh less on the moon.

Ⓑ her spacesuit makes her weigh more on the moon.

Ⓒ she weighs less on the moon than she would on Earth.

Ⓓ she weighs more on the moon than she would on Earth.

3. When Jacky plays outside on the moon, she must make sure she does not

Ⓐ jump too high. Ⓒ leave footprints.

Ⓑ get rained on. Ⓓ get a rip in her spacesuit.

4. Look at the calendars below. Which one shows the day that Neil Armstrong walked on the moon?

Ⓐ
June 1969						
S	M	T	W	Th	F	S
1	2	3	4	5	6	7
8	9	10	11	12	13	14
15	16	17	18	19	20	21
22	23	24	25	26	27	28
29	30					

Ⓑ
July 1969						
S	M	T	W	Th	F	S
		1	2	3	4	5
6	7	8	9	10	11	12
13	14	15	16	17	18	19
20	21	22	23	24	25	26
27	28	29	30	31		

Ⓒ
July 1969						
S	M	T	W	Th	F	S
		1	2	3	4	5
6	7	8	9	10	11	12
13	14	15	16	17	18	19
20	21	22	23	24	25	26
27	28	29	30	31		

5. Look at the picture to the right. Which story does it show?

Ⓐ "The First Step"

Ⓑ "Jumping Jacky"

All Over the Earth

What covers most of the Earth? Is it land? No, it is not land. Is it water? Yes, it is! Ocean water covers most of the Earth.

One ocean is the Pacific Ocean. The Pacific is the biggest ocean. It is the deepest ocean. Lots of islands are in the Pacific Ocean.

One ocean is the Atlantic Ocean. The Atlantic is the second-biggest ocean. Lots of ships cross this ocean.

One ocean is the Indian Ocean. The Indian Ocean is the warmest ocean.

One ocean is the Arctic Ocean. The Arctic is the smallest ocean. It is the coldest ocean.

The Wet Hat

Ms. Day said, "The Red Sea is part of the Indian Ocean. Parts of the Red Sea are very hot. How hot are they? They are so hot they can burn your skin!"

Ms. Day's students were surprised. They asked, "What part of the Red Sea is so hot? Why is it so hot?"

Ms. Day said, "Some bottom parts are very hot. They are hot because of volcanoes in the area. The volcanoes let out heat."

"Now," said Ms. Day, "I drop a blue hat into the Red Sea. What does it become?"

"Wet!" said the students.

Directions: Fill in the bubble next to each correct answer.

1. From the stories, you can tell that

Ⓐ seas are parts of oceans.

Ⓑ only blue hats can become wet.

Ⓒ ships do not cross the Red Sea.

Ⓓ volcanic activity makes water cold.

2. Which ocean is the second-biggest ocean?

Ⓐ Arctic Ocean

Ⓑ Indian Ocean

Ⓒ Pacific Ocean

Ⓓ Atlantic Ocean

3. Which of these statements is *not* true about the Indian Ocean?

Ⓐ It is the warmest ocean.

Ⓑ The Red Sea is part of it.

Ⓒ Some of its bottom parts are very hot.

Ⓓ It is the deepest ocean.

4. Put the names of the oceans in order from smallest to biggest. Draw a big "1" over the name of the largest ocean. Draw a big "4" over the name of the smallest ocean. Use a blue crayon.

| Arctic Ocean | Atlantic Ocean | Indian Ocean | Pacific Ocean |

5. Look at the picture to the right. Which story does it show?

Ⓐ "All Over the Earth"

Ⓑ "The Wet Hat"

Nonfiction

Twisting Your Tongue

You can read the words "toy" and "boat." It is easy to say each word. It is easy to say each word fast.

Now try to say the words together. Try to say them together five times fast!

toy boat, toy boat, toy boat, toy boat, toy boat

Most likely, you could not do it. Your sounds did not come out right.

Together, the words "toy" and "boat" make up a tongue twister. Tongue twisters are words that you cannot say over and over fast. If you try, your tongue will feel like it is all twisted up!

Fiction

Food for Thought

Claire said, "Try to say 'a box of biscuits' five times as fast as you can. I do not think you can. I think you will make a mistake."

Henry tried. He made many mistakes. Henry said, "Now it is your turn. Try to say, 'She sells seashells by the seashore' five times fast."

Claire and Henry both tried to say the tongue twisters. They laughed at their mistakes. Claire said, "Let's stop. Let's go eat fresh figs and cheap sheep soup."

Henry said, "We can eat fresh figs and cheap sheep soup, but we can't *say* them fast!"

Directions: Fill in the bubble next to each correct answer.

1. **The words "toy" and "boat" make up a tongue twister**
   Ⓐ when you say each word quickly.
   Ⓑ when you say each word slowly.
   Ⓒ when you say the words together once.
   Ⓓ when you say the words together quickly many times.

2. **What did Henry and Claire do when they made mistakes?**
   Ⓐ laughed   Ⓒ twisted their tongues
   Ⓑ ate fresh figs   Ⓓ stopped to get biscuits

3. **What did you read about in both stories?**
   Ⓐ toy boats   Ⓒ cheap sheep
   Ⓑ word sounds   Ⓓ fast tongues

4. **Say the words in each box five times fast. Is it a tongue twister? If so, color the box blue.**

   | figs | fresh figs | cheap | sheep soup | cheap sheep soup |

5. **Look at the picture to the right. Which story does it show?**

   Ⓐ "Twisting Your Tongue"

   Ⓑ "Food for Thought"

toy boat,
toi boit,
tow but,
tal bat...

Nonfiction

An Author's Guests

Jean Craighead George is a famous writer. She writes books for children. Many of her books are about animals. One time, one of Jean's books got a big prize. Jean was excited. She was so excited, she did something silly. She meant to give her guest cookies. She gave her visitor dog food instead!

One time, Jean had a small falcon. A falcon is a kind of bird. A falcon eats meat. It hunts small animals. Jean's falcon flew in the house. Where did it land? First, it landed in a bowl of jelly. Then it landed on a guest's head!

Fiction

Out of Sight

Laura said, "Hurry up! We can't be late. We don't want to miss the big game. The Lions and the Falcons are playing. It should be a great game!"

Scott said, "I know! I am so excited. I just need to find my hat so my head won't get cold while we watch the game. Oh, where could it be? It is not on my bed. It's not under my pillow. It's not in my closet. I have looked everywhere! I don't see it anywhere!"

Laura looked at Scott. She laughed, "Scott, you can't see it, but I can. It is on your head!"

Scott stopped. "Oh. Well, let's go then! I have everything I need."

Directions: Fill in the bubble next to each correct answer.

1. **What do both stories have in common?**
   - Ⓐ They both are about excited people.
   - Ⓑ They both are about exciting games.
   - Ⓒ They both are about excited falcons.
   - Ⓓ They both are about exciting guests.

2. **Where did Jean's falcon land first?**
   - Ⓐ on a big prize
   - Ⓑ on a guest's head
   - Ⓒ in a bowl of jelly
   - Ⓓ in a bowl of dog food

3. **From both stories, one can tell that**
   - Ⓐ Scott was excited to be Laura's guest.
   - Ⓑ Jean would have been excited to go to a game.
   - Ⓒ the Falcons are the most exciting team to watch.
   - Ⓓ excited people can sometimes do silly things.

4. **Where did Scott find his hat?**

   Ⓐ on his  | Ⓑ under his 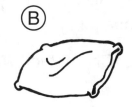 | Ⓒ on his

5. **Look at the picture to the right. Which story does it show?**

   - Ⓐ "An Author's Guests"

   - Ⓑ "Out of Sight"

Four Thumbs and a Pouch

Some people call koalas "koala bears." The truth is that koalas are not bears. Koalas are not like bears at all. Koalas have pouches. Koalas carry their babies in their pouches. Bears do not have pouches.

Koalas live in Australia. They live in trees. You have two thumbs. You have one thumb on each hand. Koalas have four thumbs. They have two thumbs on each hand. The extra thumbs help koalas hold on tight to the trees when the wind blows.

Pizza for Breakfast

Craig told his sister, "Koalas only eat one thing. They only eat the leaves of eucalyptus trees. I am going to be like a koala. I am going to eat only one thing."

Craig's sister said, "Oh, brother. What is this one thing you are going to eat?"

"I am only going to eat pizza," Craig announced.

So Craig ate pizza for breakfast. He ate pizza for lunch. He ate pizza for dinner. Then he had a nice slice of pizza for dessert. Craig liked pizza. He was happy.

Craig ate only pizza for days. After one week, Craig was sick of pizza. He said, "I don't want to be like a koala. I want to eat yogurt and rice. I want to eat vegetables and fruit. I want to eat anything that is *not* pizza!"

Directions: Fill in the bubble next to each correct answer.

1. **What was in both stories?**

   Ⓐ pizza   Ⓒ thumbs

   Ⓑ koalas   Ⓓ leaves

2. **When did Ben get sick of pizza?**

   Ⓐ after lunch   Ⓒ after one week

   Ⓑ after dinner   Ⓓ after breakfast

3. **A fact is true. A fact is not made up. "Pizza for Breakfast" is a made-up story, but it has a true fact. Which answer is a true fact?**

   Ⓐ Koalas only eat eucalyptus leaves.

   Ⓑ Ben likes to eat eucalyptus leaves.

   Ⓒ Koalas like to eat pizza for breakfast.

   Ⓓ Ben has the same number of thumbs as a koala.

4. **Look at the hands. Write "koala" or "person" below each hand. Write a big "T" on each thumb.**

      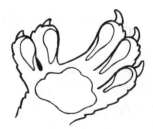

   _____   _____

   - - - - - - - - - - - - - -   - - - - - - - - - - - - - -

   _____   _____

5. **Look at the picture to the right. Which story does it show?**

   Ⓐ "Four Thumbs and a Pouch"

   Ⓑ "Pizza for Breakfast"

A Snowy Save

Andrea was playing in the snow. She got cold and started to walk home. A big wind blew. The wind blew Andrea into a pile of snow. Andrea was buried! She was buried up to her chest!

Andrea tried to get out. She could not move. She was trapped by the snow. Andrea called for help. No one could hear her. No one could see her. There was too much wind and too much snow.

Only the neighbor's dog Villa heard Andrea. Villa jumped over her fence. She found Andrea. As Andrea held onto Villa's neck, Villa pulled. She pulled and pulled. She pulled Andrea out!

Fiction

The Free Ride

Juan started down the steep hill. His sled went fast in the snow! Then Juan saw something in his way. It was a big dog! Juan couldn't stop. His sled was going too fast.

Juan was afraid there was going to be a big crash. He closed his eyes. Suddenly, Juan felt something warm. The big dog was sitting on Juan's lap! It had been knocked onto the sled.

At the bottom of the steep hill, the dog grabbed the sled rope. It started to pull the sled up the hill. The dog wanted to go for another downhill ride!

Directions: Fill in the bubble next to each correct answer.

1. **What did you read about in both stories?**

   (A) a dog   (C) a hill

   (B) a sled   (D) a wind

2. **How did Andrea get buried up to her chest in the snow?**

   (A) She was playing in a pile of snow.

   (B) Villa pulled her into a pile of snow.

   (C) The wind blew her into a pile of snow.

   (D) She got cold and fell into a pile of snow.

3. **Why didn't Juan stop when he saw the dog?**

   (A) His eyes were closed.   (C) His sled was going too fast.

   (B) His sled was going to crash.   (D) The dog was too fast.

4. **Look at the information from the first story. What is missing? What should go in the empty box?**

   | Andrea called for help. | → | | → | Villa pulled Andrea out! |

   (A) Andrea was playing in the snow.

   (B) Andrea fell into a deep pile of snow.

   (C) Andrea held onto Villa's neck.

   (D) Juan saw a big dog in his way.

5. **Look at the picture to the right. Which story does it show?**

   (A) "A Snowy Save"

   (B) "The Free Ride"

Fresh from the Ocean

A girl was in Bahrain. Bahrain is a country. The girl had a jar. She walked out into the ocean. She filled her jar. She filled it with water.

What was the water for? The water was for drinking. But ocean water is salty! You cannot drink salty water! You would become very sick. So how could the water in the jar be for drinking?

In some places, fresh water bubbles up. The fresh water is under the sea bed. The fresh water makes a pocket. It makes a pocket of fresh water in salty water. The water in the jar was not salty. It was fresh.

A Letter About Long Ago

Dear Franklin,

Long ago, people in my country put wax in their ears! The people who did this were divers. They dove deep into the ocean. The wax protected their ears.

You may ask what the people diving for. They were diving for pearls. It was a dangerous thing to do. The divers had to watch out for sharks. They had to watch out for sea snakes. They had to watch out for jellyfish.

Please tell me what people did in your country.

Your pen pal from Bahrain,

Ali

Directions: Fill in the bubble next to each correct answer.

1. **Where did the fresh water in the jar come from?**

   (A) under the sea bed

   (B) under the salt bed

   (C) under the sea bubble

   (D) under the salt bubble

2. **It did not say in Ali's letter that the divers had to watch out for**

   (A) sharks.

   (B) stingrays.

   (C) jellyfish.

   (D) sea snakes.

3. **Both stories are about**

   (A) diving.

   (B) pearls.

   (C) Bahrain.

   (D) fresh water.

4. **A letter has a greeting and a closing. The greeting begins the letter. It is like saying "hello" to the person receiving the letter. The closing ends the letter. It is like saying "goodbye." What was the greeting in Ali's letter?**

   (A) Please tell me what people did in your country.

   (B) Your pen pal from Bahrain

   (C) Ali

   (D) Dear Franklin,

5. **Look at the picture to the right. Which story does it show?**

   (A) "Fresh from the Ocean"

   (B) "A Letter About Long Ago"

Everything Floats

A boy jumped into the water. The water was deep. The boy could not swim. He was not wearing a life vest. The boy did not sink. He could not sink. He floated. How come?

The boy had jumped into the Dead Sea. The Dead Sea is very salty. It is so salty that people cannot sink in it. They float.

The Dead Sea is really a deep lake. It is a low, salt lake. The Dead Sea is below sea level. It is in Israel.

A Tricky Egg

Paul said, "I can do a magic trick. Watch me, Callie! Watch me do my magic trick."

Paul picked up an egg. He said, "Watch me while I make this egg float."

Callie watched as Paul waved his hand over the egg. Then Paul dropped the egg into a glass of water. The egg did not sink! It floated!

Callie said, "I know you only waved your hand for show. How did you really get the egg to float?"

Paul said, "I added lots and lots of salt to the water."

"That's a good trick!" said Callie.

Practice 17 – Questions

Directions: Fill in the bubble next to each correct answer.

1. Both stories are about

(A) tricking people.

(B) people who cannot sink.

(C) water that is below sea level.

(D) what happens in very salty water.

2. Jake's egg floated because

(A) it was magic.

(B) Kelly was tricked.

(C) the water was salty.

(D) Jake waved his hand.

3. Oceans are salty. People can sink in the ocean. Most likely this is because

(A) most oceans are not as salty as the Dead Sea.

(B) Jake did not wave his hand over the ocean.

(C) the Dead Sea is not as salty as the ocean.

(D) Jake did not add lots of salt to the ocean.

4. Read the sentence below. Circle the two words that are wrong. Write the correct words on the line below.

The Dead Sea is really a shallow ocean.

_____   _____

-     -

_____   _____

5. Look at the picture to the right. Which story does it show?

(A) "Everything Floats"

(B) "A Tricky Egg"

Nonfiction

The Chinese New Year

China is a big country. A lot of people live in China. The people in China celebrate the New Year. The Chinese New Year is when a new moon comes. This happens between January 21 and February 19.

How do people celebrate the Chinese New Year? They eat good food. They play games. They have fun. They talk. They laugh. They set off firecrackers.

Red is an important color during this time. People wear red clothes. They hang up red papers. They paint their doors red. The color red is everywhere. Red is the color of the New Year.

Fiction

The Red Doors

A bad beast came at the end of every year. It came to villages in China. The beast did bad things. It ate the villager's animals. The villagers fought the beast, but it always came back.

The villagers found out something. They found out the beast did not like light. It did not like noise. It did not like the color red.

At the end of the year, the villagers lit a big bonfire. They lit lots of firecrackers. They painted the doors of their homes red. The beast was scared by the light, the noise, and the red doors. It ran away.

Directions: Fill in the bubble next to each correct answer.

1. **What did you read about in both stories?**

   Ⓐ a big beast

   Ⓑ the new moon

   Ⓒ the color red

   Ⓓ a bad country

2. **What was *not* true about the beast from the second story?**

   Ⓐ It lit lots of firecrackers.

   Ⓑ It did not like the color red.

   Ⓒ It ate the villager's animals.

   Ⓓ It came at the end of every year.

3. **Most likely, red is the color of the New Year because**

   Ⓐ firecrackers make a lot of noise.

   Ⓑ people painted the doors of their homes red.

   Ⓒ the New Year comes when there is a new moon.

   Ⓓ it is said that the color red scared the beast.

4. **Look at these dates. Which ones could be a day when the new moon comes in China? Color those boxes red. Don't color the other boxes.**

February 12	February 15	January 16	January 25	February 28

5. **Look at the picture to the right. Which story does it show?**

   Ⓐ "The Chinese New Year"

   Ⓑ "The Red Doors"

Sailing Across Land

Antarctica is a continent. It is big, but not many people live there. This is because it is so cold. Antarctica is covered with ice.

Borge Ousland was all alone. He crossed Antarctica. No one had ever crossed Antarctica alone before. It was too cold. It was too far. There was no one to help on the way.

How did Borge cross? He used skis. He pulled a sled. He also had sails! He tied the sails to his body. The sails would fill with air. They helped him go fast. The sails helped him pull his heavy sled.

Birds that Swim

Jess said, "Did you know that there is a bird that cannot fly? It's true! This bird cannot fly, but it can swim. Some of these birds stay in the water for a long time. They stay in the water for five months!"

Bobby said, "Where can I see a bird like that?"

Jess said, "These birds live in Antarctica. I will take you to see one."

Bobby said, "You can't take me to Antarctica!"

Jess said, "I can't take you to Antarctica, but I can take you to the zoo! We will see penguins at the zoo. We will see penguins from Antarctica."

Directions: Fill in the bubble next to each correct answer.

1. **What did Borge do that no one else had ever done before?**
   (A) He crossed Antarctica alone.
   (B) He used skies to go fast on ice.
   (C) He pulled a heavy sled in the cold.
   (D) He tied sails that would fill with air to his body.

2. **How long do some penguins stay in the water?**
   (A) 2 months   (C) 4 months
   (B) 3 months   (D) 5 months

3. **From the stories, you can tell that Borge**
   (A) could have swum across Antarctica.
   (B) could have seen penguins in Antarctica.
   (C) could have gone to the zoo in Antarctica.
   (D) could have talked to Ryan about Antarctica.

4. **Look at the word "Antarctica." How many of each letter can you find in "Antarctica"? The first one has been done for you.**

A	N	T	A	R	C	T	I	C	A

   A ------ 3 ------   C ---------------   T ---------------

5. **Look at the picture to the right. Which story does it show?**

   (A) "Sailing Across Land"

   (B) "Birds that Swim"

Saved by the Bell

Don was on a bike. He was on his ranch. He was looking after his cows. There was a sick calf that needed his help. Don was busy looking for that young calf. He didn't notice an angry bull coming toward him.

Suddenly, Don was hit! The angry bull hit him. The bull knocked Don off his bike. It began to step on Don.

Don could not do anything. The bull was too angry and too big. Then Don heard a bell. The bell was on Don's lead cow, Daisy. All the other cows followed Daisy and her bell.

Daisy ran to Don. All the other cows followed. Daisy pushed the bull away. Then, she and the other cows made a circle around Don. They kept Don safe from the bull.

The Country Horses

Kia lived in the city. She went to the country to visit her friend Sally. Kia saw some animals. The animals were black and white. They said, "Moo."

Kia started to laugh. She said, "Country horses are strange. They do not look like the city horses policemen ride. City horses say 'neigh.' They do not say 'moo.'"

Betty started to laugh. She said, "You are not looking at a horse. You are looking at a cow! The cows are milk cows. The milk you buy in the city comes from cows in the country."

Directions: Fill in the bubble next to each correct answer.

1. **What is *not* true about Daisy?**

   Ⓐ Daisy had a bell.

   Ⓑ Daisy was Don's lead cow.

   Ⓒ The other cows followed Daisy.

   Ⓓ Daisy knocked Don off of his bike.

2. **Why did Kia go to the country?**

   Ⓐ to buy some milk   Ⓒ to look at some animals

   Ⓑ to visit her friend   Ⓓ to hear a horse say "moo"

3. **From the stories, you can tell that most likely**

   Ⓐ a policeman rode Daisy.   Ⓒ Don lived in the country.

   Ⓑ Sally rode a motorbike.   Ⓓ Kia had seen cows before.

4. **Draw lines to match the people words on the left to the animal words on the right.**

   boy   calf

   girl   cow

   baby   bull

5. **Look at the picture to the right. Which story does it show?**

   Ⓐ "Saved by the Bell"

   Ⓑ "The Country Horses"

Archie's Pet

Archie Roosevelt was sick. He had to stay in bed. He was not happy. His brothers said, "Archie's pet will make him happy. We will bring his pet to him."

Archie lived in the White House. He lived there 100 years ago. He lived there when his father, Theodore Roosevelt, was president of the United States.

Archie's pet was a pony. Archie's brothers snuck the pony into the White House! They snuck it into the elevator!

The pony did not want to get out. It liked being in the elevator. There was a mirror in the elevator. The pony did not want to stop looking in the mirror!

The Monster Upstairs

"We can't go up the stairs!" said Mateo. "There is a real monster up there."

Ron said, "We will be brave. We will go up the stairs. We won't be afraid."

The two boys started up the stairs. They went slowly. Then, they saw it! It was a monster! It had two heads! The monster was coming closer and closer!

The boys didn't run away. The boys started to laugh. The boys laughed because the monster was not a monster! There was an old mirror at the top of the stairs. The boys were seeing themselves!

Directions: Fill in the bubble next to each correct answer.

1. **What did you read about in both stories?**

   Ⓐ a pony   Ⓒ a monster

   Ⓑ a mirror   Ⓓ an elevator

2. **The monster**

   Ⓐ was not old.   Ⓒ was not slow.

   Ⓑ was not real.   Ⓓ was not brave.

3. **Why didn't the pony want to get out of the elevator?**

   Ⓐ He did not want to stay in bed.

   Ⓑ He did not want to make Archie happy.

   Ⓒ He did not want to stop looking in the mirror.

   Ⓓ He did not want to be snuck into the White House.

4. **Fill in the blanks to complete these sentences.**

   - Archie's _____ was a pony.

   - Archie lived in the _____ House.

   - Archie's _____ was the president of the U.S.

5. **Look at the picture to the right. Which story does it show?**

   Ⓐ "Archie's Pet"

   Ⓑ "The Monster Upstairs"

Nonfiction

Reading with Fingers

Louis Braille was blind. He could not see. He could not see pages. He could not see letters. Still, Louis was able to read.

How could Louis read if he could not see pages? How could he read if he could not see letters? How could he read if he could not use his eyes?

Louis could not see the letters, but he could feel them! Louis invented an alphabet. The alphabet was made of dots. Each letter was a different pattern of six dots. The dots were raised. Louis could feel the raised dots. Louis could read by using his fingers!

Fiction

Reading in the Dark

A big storm hit. Strong winds blew. Trees were knocked over. Zack said, "The power and lights are out. The computer isn't working. It is dark in the house. We can't watch T.V. What are we going to do?"

Zack's Uncle Phil said, "Let's read. I know a good story you will like."

Zack said, "Uncle Phil, I can't read. It is too dark."

Uncle Phil said, "I can read to you. My books are printed in the Braille alphabet."

Zack said, "That's right! I can't read in the dark, but you can! Uncle Phil, you can read in the dark and the light."

Directions: Fill in the bubble next to each correct answer.

1. How could Louis read?

(A) by using his eyes   (C) by seeing the letters

(B) by seeing the pages   (D) by feeling raised dots

2. What is *not* true after the big storm hit?

(A) It was dark.   (C) The power was out.

(B) The computer worked.   (D) The lights were out.

3. From the stories, you can tell that

(A) Zack cannot use his fingers to read.

(B) Louis did not know any good stories.

(C) Uncle Phil can see pages and letters.

(D) Louis read stories when the power was out.

4. Put these four parts from the second story in the correct order. Put a "1" by the story part that came first. Put a "4" by the story part that came last.

_____ "Let's read. I know a good story."

_____ "I can read to you. My books are printed in the Braille alphabet."

_____ "Uncle Phil, I can't read. It's too dark."

_____ "The power and lights are out."

5. Look at the picture to the right. Which story does it show?

(A) "Reading with Fingers"

(B) "Reading in the Dark"

Answer Key

Practice 1 Questions (page 5)
1. A
2. B
3. C
4. B
5. B

Practice 2 Questions (page 7)
1. D
2. B
3. C
4. C
5. B

Practice 3 Questions (page 9)
1. C
2. B
3. D
4. A
5. A

Practice 4 Questions (page 11)
1. A
2. B
3. A
4. *(possible answers)* month: August; year: 2010, 1926; country: England, France
5. A

Practice 5 Questions (page 13)
1. D
2. B
3. A
4. C
5. B

Practice 6 Questions (page 15)
1. A
2. D
3. B
4. right, left
5. B

Practice 7 Questions (page 17)
1. C
2. D
3. A
4. *(possible answers)* huge: tiny, small; small: huge, big; strong: weak
5. B

Practice 8 Questions (page 19)
1. B
2. C
3. D
4. out
5. B

Practice 9 Questions (page 21)
1. C
2. B
3. D
4. 1st: Pam; 2nd: Pam's brother; 3rd: a lady on the beach
5. A

Practice 10 Questions (page 23)
1. A
2. C
3. D
4. C
5. B

Practice 11 Questions (page 25)
1. A
2. D
3. D
4. Arctic (4), Atlantic (2), Indian (3), Pacific (1)
5. B

Practice 12 Questions (page 27)
1. D
2. A
3. B
4. *colored boxes:* fresh figs, sheep soup, cheap sheep soup
5. A

Practice 13 Questions (page 29)
1. A
2. C
3. D
4. C
5. B

Practice 14 Questions (page 31)
1. B
2. C
3. A
4. person, 1 thumb; koala, 2 thumbs
5. B

Practice 15 Questions (page 33)
1. A
2. C
3. C
4. C
5. A

Practice 16 Questions (page 35)
1. A
2. B
3. C
4. D
5. A

Practice 17 Questions (page 37)
1. D
2. C
3. A
4. *circled words:* shallow ocean; *correction:* deep lake
5. B

Practice 18 Questions (page 39)
1. C
2. A
3. D
4. *colored boxes:* February 12, February 15, January 25
5. B

Practice 19 Questions (page 41)
1. A
2. D
3. B
4. A (3), C (2), T (2)
5. A

Practice 20 Questions (page 43)
1. D
2. B
3. C
4. boy, bull; girl, cow; baby, calf
5. A

Practice 21 Questions (page 45)
1. B
2. B
3. C
4. pet, White, father
5. B

Practice 22 Questions (page 47)
1. D
2. B
3. A
4. 2, 4, 3, 1
5. B